# The Amazing Monarch

written by Bruce Goldstone

McGraw-Hill
School Division

New York          Farmington

Look up! A bright orange-and-black butterfly cloud flutters in the air. Listen. You aren't hearing the wind blowing through the trees. It is the soft beating of thousands of wings.

At the end of March millions of orange-and-black monarch butterflies are returning from their winter rest. The butterflies are looking for milkweed plants on which to lay their eggs.

Monarch butterflies have lived in North America for two million years. This is their story.

The journey of the monarch begins in a silent milkweed field like this one. Beginning at the end of August, for two to five weeks, monarch butterflies lay about 700 eggs each. That means a single field of milkweed can hold thousands and thousands of eggs. Each egg is no bigger than the head of a pin.

About four days after a monarch egg is laid, a tiny caterpillar hatches from it. The caterpillars are so small that twenty-five of them lined up head to tail would measure only an inch. Now that's small!

Like all insects, caterpillars have no bones, not even ribs. All these tiny insects do is eat. The first thing that a caterpillar eats is its own empty egg shell. Next, the leaves of the milkweed plant offer them a tasty treat. The caterpillars eat leaf after leaf and grow larger and larger every day.

The caterpillars grow so quickly that they outgrow their own skin. When they get rid of the old one, the new skin underneath is soft and fragile. But soon the skin hardens into a tough outer layer. Monarch caterpillars shed their skins five times.

The caterpillars take two weeks to reach full size. Soon they are about two inches long. They are eight times longer and 2,500 times heavier than when they were born!

Now most of the caterpillars are ready to change again. Each one spins a silk mat onto something strong, such as a branch or stem. Then the caterpillar hangs upside down from the mat. It gets rid of its last skin, and becomes a light-green chrysalis (kris ´ə lis).

The chrysalis looks still and quiet. But inside, amazing changes are taking place. A caterpillar has sixteen legs and a mouth that can eat leaves. Inside the chrysalis, it changes into a butterfly with six legs, four wings, and a mouth that can drink liquids from flowers.

When it is almost time for the butterfly to come out of its chrysalis, you can see the orange-and-black pattern of the monarch inside it.

After five to fifteen days, the butterflies are ready to hatch. Each butterfly opens the chrysalis with its head. The chrysalis breaks apart and the new butterfly comes out.

At first, butterfly wings are soft and wet. A newly hatched butterfly hangs from a branch for a few hours. When the wings dry, the adult butterfly can fly.